# In Time to Tango

## by

## ARDEN TICE

## NICHOLS SANDS

Introduction by Belinda Subraman

Preface by JoAnn Fineman, M.D.

**FIRST EDITION 2002**
ISBN: 0-935839-23-2

PUBLISHED BY:
**VERGIN PRESS**
P.O. Box 370322
El Paso, Texas 79937

Cover painting © by Dan Griggs of New Mexico is titled, "21st
Century Cotillion." Griggs is known for paintings that express the
mystery of time and place and the complexity of human desire and
experience.

The following poems appeared in the anthology, *Scenes*, from the *Live Poets Society*, Santa Fe, New Mexico, December 2001: "words in our teeth," "in the beginning," "we are all afraid of the night," "we each had a sweet dream," "I was leaving," "this emblazoned October," "what does it matter," "out other lives winding down," "winding the road to angel fire," "the watermelon morning," (Arden Tice).

The poems "My Son, My Son Calls" and "Kurosawa dreamed mutated dandelions" were published in *The Augmented Moon*. "Moon Memories" was published in *A Naming of Women* (Arden Tice).

The poems "Child of War" and "Names" were published in *Rio Grande Writers Quarterly* (Nichols Sands).

"Names" was also published in *Poetry and the Vietnam Experience*, David B. Steinman Festival of the Arts, St. Lawrence University (Nichols Sands).

"Child of War" and "To Wendell Berry" were published in *LIFE FISH*; selected poems 1986 from the Artist-in-Residence Program, VA Medical Center, Albuquerque, NM (Nichols Sands).

# INTRODUCTION

I have known Arden since 1990. I have seen her go through many changes, always searching, searching for comfort, peace... meaning. I'm sure she could say the same of me as well. We shared in each other's eccentricities through poetry and conversation. We went through a gamut of feelings about each other, our loved ones, and ourselves. We did our own sort of dance until we finally struck a deep chord of meaning and became true friends.

*In Time To Tango* is the story of a mature man and woman who have led full and dramatic lives. They bear very deep and painful scars from sudden unjustifiable, unexpected deaths that shocked their senses. They have embarked on a brave process to learn to manage their pain, to work daily to grow with and through it. Even braver, they work on a relationship to keep it alive and sustaining for both.

I am struck by the wisdom of these two poets. Nick writes: *It IS for you, / The swallows fly. // If you are so far away / You cannot see them, // Is that the swallow's fault?* Arden recognizes: *what does it matter if my love / is a mixed / blessing / combining as I do father / son lover / as long as I know how the lines intersect / as long as I don't expect / from you / a permanent rainbow / a pot of gold.*

To have found one another was a gift. Their effort to nurture one another and the evident growth in their relationship is nothing short of admirable. It is a testimony to what real love can do. It is not simply pleasure based, but soul based.

The push and pull of the tango is indeed true life. All relationships are push and pull, but to hold on to one another, in good times and bad, is the highest form of commitment. *In Time to Tango* demonstrates Arden and Nick plan to finish the dance.

Belinda Subraman,
poet, author, editor

## PREFACE

This poem uses the metaphor of the Argentine Tango to shape its' form and to give a construction which fits admirably with the content and the evoked experience of the poem. It is, indeed, a dance between two narrators, together and yet separated and apart — as the introduction says, each face one another but look into infinity — repeatedly in rhythm together but embedded in a tension which is always there. That is the nature of this narrative poem, which sustains the tension to its' ending, although with some hint that each narrator will find a new and different self after the "dance."

As a psychoanalyst, both intrigued and frequently puzzled by the creative act, in whatever medium it is expressed, I read and ponder this poem both as a work of art and as a creative act emerging from grief, anger and the overwhelming experience of sudden and never quite reparable loss.

In the prologue, the narrator whom I shall call the mother-narrator, experiences herself as the dead son, seeing herself as "carried forward into the crematorium," and merges with the lost child "to join my son in the flames." Such is the immediate response to such a catastrophic event-breaking down the usual barriers to cope and control the outer world and the inner response to it. The outer world collapses and the only immediate source of survival is to freeze, contain movement and words, as though to hold the body together within the skin.

Both narrators experience this and begin to slowly put the inner world into tentative words, to each other and to themselves.

The healing attempt — to tell the story — to have the listening audience hear and know, is the origin of creativity and the act of making something new and novel out of an inner void and rage against consciousness. The beginning of mourning is to shape words which tell the story, and carry the rage and sorrow. When the narrator as mother says she wants to "beat a tambourine, beat a drum," she is telling us of the first attempt to make angry, wordless noise, before words can be shaped. When the words finally come, in the poem, there is something tangible, "a result of the pleasure and the pain."

The merged relationship between loss, mourning and creativity here speaks for itself. While all creative acts possibly cannot be linked to loss and the attempt to repair and reconstruct the self, many if not most can, I believe.

Of course, there must be a word capability which allows the regression necessary to feel and construct, but with the constant ability to flow between the conscious and formatting mind and the unconscious or pre-conscious levels of the mind and never become embedded or stuck in either. It is this flow between conscious and knowing and the unstructured unconscious which allows the creative experience to be communicated and formed.

In the body of the poem, both narrative voices identify themselves with the lost dead—the warrior narrator sees himself as dead and abandoned by the Lieutenant in the safety of tree cover, the mother-lover narrator wants to give everything yet can't give enough. It is possible that this narrator herself can never be given the real gift of her restored son. In both narrations, it becomes clear that everyone around both of the "dancers" join the conspiracy to suppress and stifle words; they never allow the past and the dead son or the dead or maimed victims of the warrior narrator to exist.

The warrior narrator as lover,can imagine and experience closeness but then is overcome and frightened by the intimacy of loving.

Both narrative voices hover on the edge of the safety of loving and, even if briefly, yielding wholeheartedly to the other, yet, as in the recurrent metaphor of the tango, draw back into the internal past and the aloneness which seems to engulf them, much as the dancer themselves strain apart but remain in tandem and moving harmony. The warrior narrator is angry, enraged and cannot find the direct target of his anger-anger as a felt inner experience needs a target to resolve itself, not in actuality, but in the conscious fantasy of the one who holds the anger. In war — there is always a target: persons, animals, the enemy and the outer world in whatever form.

After many years the warrior narrator realizes he can attack the Lieutenant with words as his missiles, to then form a poetic image of his rage.

The mother narrator, as the death anniversary approaches, begins to push against the "enormity" of the destruction and a glimpse of the "alien" self emerges, she is still here. This illuminates the heart of the transformation of loss and mourning into an act of new creation. The capacity to tolerate the self as survivor is as agonizing as the letting go of the lost person, yet as both take place, the survivor begins to reconstitute a new inner image of the self, flawed and altered, but "still here."

The sharing of the secret, unspoken, becomes more bearable when the two narrators can hear and be heard , with the act of converting the inner world into an outer form — words, images, movement, as in the dance. This becomes the inception of the transformation of some of the grief into a creative product and act. The mother narrator and the warrior narrator begin to shape and give form to their inner worlds, together. In creativity after loss, the "audience" is always ultimately the self since the task of creativity as a reparation is the task of altering the self by externalizing to the hearing, feeling other as audience; and creating and reconstructing a different self. The created self after loss is never the former self, the act of making something new from the old is both to relinquish, and to restore. In this work, both narrators never quite allow us to see them firmly together, or never apart. Their work is to continue the dance, as with all human beings after the devastation of loss and trauma, a dance which will continue after the music stops.

Jo Ann B. Fineman MD

## ACKNOWLEDGMENT

Our thanks and appreciation to Jonathan Shay, M.D., for his encouragement and for his book, *Achilles in Vietnam,* to Judith Herman, author of *Trauma and Recovery*, and to Robert Nolen, a member of our writing group, for his excellent critiquing and support. We also want to thank all of our other teachers of the dance.

Dedicated to
those touching
and transforming
sorrow

14

# TABLE OF CONTENTS

## Prolog: Before the Dance

*my son calls* ............................................................... 22

*Moon Memories* ........................................................ 24

*Kurosawa dreamed mutated dandelions* ................... 26

*B. says sharply to me,*

    *"Did you hear, do you know?"* ............................ 28

Child of War ................................................................. 30

Names ........................................................................... 32

To Wendell Berry .......................................................... 34

It has taken me thirty years .......................................... 35

## In Time to Tango

*The Argentine Tango, a hybrid* ................................... 39

*In the beginning* ........................................................ 41

*words in our teeth* ..................................................... 42

Looking into the Milky Way ........................................... 43

*we are all afraid of the night* .................................... 45

I desertman of the dry sea ............................................ 47

16

*an owl came to my balcony* ............................................. 49

Brooding and dark in ............................................. 52

*we each had a sweet dream* ............................................. 54

I have hitched my Wagon to your Star ............................................. 55

*moving on* ............................................. 56

Take this rock wall ............................................. 57

*Maria, comes over* ............................................. 59

Do not ask me why ............................................. 60

*In 1968 the outside world* ............................................. 64

*morning rays fill the scotch* ............................................. 65

in the morning when your eyes are soft ............................................. 67

*I was leaving* ............................................. 68

If you'll be my lily pad ............................................. 69

*this emblazoned october* ............................................. 70

The weld is stronger than either side ............................................. 72

*what does it matter* ............................................. 73

I need to communicate ............................................. 74

*perhaps you believe* ............................................. 75

Perhaps, I do not speak aloud ............................................. 76

*Driving on the mountain road* ............................................. 77

*our other lives winding down* ............................................. 79

*Before I went to sleep last night* ........................................ 81

*winding the road to angel fire* ........................................ 82

By your own hand ........................................ 83

*the watermelon morning* ........................................ 84

Old Gold ........................................ 85

*shards of memory* ........................................ 86

# Prolog:
# Before the Dance

20

*Before they met she spoke in Tongues,*
*a broken language:*

*my son calls as*

*I descend down into the depths*
*the room disappears    he disappears*

*words appear    don't come near*
*lost inside nothing can rise*

*slipping away from a congealed overlay*
*drama that will never touch    cover    come near the*
*pain*

*he is dead    and I am dead ripped apart from the*
*    life I bore*
*like the naked young woman carried forward into*
*    the crematorium*

*carried in the arms of some anonymous man*
*carried toward the brick building*

*carried lightly    for she was slight as a young child*
*her dark hair flowing*

*her eyes bright and glowing*
*may they   my eyes   haunt you who live*
     *forever haunt   you*

*I am the eyes   hair flowing   body to be consumed*
     *by the flames*
*consumed in Treblinka   or here   look upon her*

*she is beautiful in her dying   look quickly*
*but never find her   she has gone away*

*look   look quickly   but never find*
*I have gone to join my son in the flames*

### moon memories

I looked out my window at five this morning
thought I saw a cold moon

I wanted it hot and haloed
don't do that   I said

a moon is a moon   you know
still I couldn't stop myself

remembering Chekhov's little man
who slept alone with his horse in the stable

he wanted to tell someone his story
he'd start

I want to tell you something
take me there   they demanded   faster faster

with the next person he'd begin again
I had a son   stop stop

I'm cold   you fool   get along   I'm late
so he'd urge his horse forward through the snow

back in the stable he leaned against the warm
flank
began to tell his horse the story

he started   I had a son
as the horse blew softly through his nostrils

the steam haloed the horse's nose
and he listened only stamping his hoofs softly

*Kurosawa dreamed mutated dandelions*

and demonmen who screamed for death
Kurosawa dreamed peach blossoms

snowing blizzards that engulfed the soul
until gentled to rest

by flowing Goddess death

I want to beat a tambourine
walk barefoot down

some unknown dirt road

I want to beat a drum
chant into the breeze

bear death joyfully upon my breast
I want to join the procession of old

*I look upon the ravaged land*
*I look into my inner scape*
*and I know we will not escape*

*I want to beat a tambourine*
*walk barefoot down the road*

*I want to beat a drum*
*chant into the breeze*

*I want to walk joyfully*
*down down into the sea*

B. says sharply to me, "Did you hear, do you know?" He drives me down the street stopping at a fire hose that blocks the road, saying only, "He's trapped, he's trapped." "What? Who?" I cry, not understanding. Someone is trapped. At the house, feeling a sudden need to move, I shake off the arm that holds me. "I'll get the child out," I say. But they push me back, tell me to sit down. I sit on the rock wall. I too am rock, silent as stone. I sit there for the child to burn so he can be taken away. A man comes to tell me they have a body. "Let me see," I mutter. I imagine Romotsky's painting of Trotsky, charred flesh and bared bone the red and black in sharp contrast. I ask, "Did he call me after the first explosion? Did he call after the second? After the gray flower blossomed, did he call as in my dreams he still calls me, and I cannot go?"

A.T.

Across time and space he
threw his voices to the universe:

## CHILD OF WAR

In the innocence of ignorance
        Of the very young,
She had come upon a trip wire,
        Tripped upon a trip wire,
        Tripped
    On a beautiful day.

We called a Medivac chopper.

The sun dappled
        Her skin and the blood.
While we worked in haste.

Only time to treat the body.

No time to treat the mind
No time to touch her soul.
No time to hold her.
Only time to smell the blood and powder.

No time to say, "I'm sorry."
No time for the lie of , "Don't worry."
No time for translators.
Only time to use all of my dressings
                         and
Only time till they took her away.

All of my time with her was gauze and blood,
        Damning the flood of her life
             on the ground.

I still don't know if she lived or died.
I never knew her name.

I can't say how much she suffered.

I can only say:

She was a child of conflict,
             A child of the war.

If you are looking for reasons.
Do you need any more?

## NAMES

Names escape the long arm of my memory.
        So much.
              So vivid.
        But not the names.


The Corporal came back to save me.
The Boy cleaned my gun and socks.
The Shark.
        I felt so good, to have won
              My first game of "Back-alley"
            That evening.
        That night a lonely mortar round
            Found a friend.
            Took him home.
The Old Woman, Mamasan three times over.
        Cursing that stray bullet.
Another Corporal, turned PFC, wouldn't take his
pill.
        and got three months off with Malaria.
The Girl cooked rice and tiny shrimp for us.
        The Taxman took the money we gave her.
            The rice too.

The Indian fired his M-60 machinegun from his
shoulder
    and helped me patch the casualties.
The Chicano from El Paso went crazy.
    Vietnam to Leavenworth.
        They called it murder.
The Friendly Village Chief was dead
    In the light of our night ambush.
The Sarge and I went up the mountain with two
PF's.
    Scared the VC off the top.
    Hunted deer on the way down.
The Shopkeeper taught me to like iced coffee
    But wouldn't tell me her name.
Rusty's name is on the Wall.
    I can't find it.
        I can't find the name.
            I can't find the names.

To Wendell Berry

You were tilling and feeling
      the Earth,
Writing your sense of smell
    Sniffing at the roots
          of regeneration.

I was in Asia,
      Human dust bowl
          in tropical paradise.

Son of a warrior,
      Sweating in the sun of war.

Only to learn the same
      So many years later.

      Thank you.

Dear Lt. W,

It has taken me thirty years to arrive at the writing of this letter. War is an angry time, but in the CAPs*, anger was simply dangerous. Our men were forced together in an extremely intimate way. I am angry with you. It sure took a long time to explode into my conscious mind. Where were you? What was this obsession with "body-counts"? I know where you were when I was pinned down. You were over in the safety of that tree-line, deciding to just leave me out there, leave me for dead. You couldn't even lift your weapon or even give the order to provide me with covering fire. I would have made the dash if you had covered me, but while I was waiting you decided I must be dead. No confirmation necessary. No need to see a body. I was always told that the Marines didn't leave any of their men behind, dead or alive. I am angry with my anger. I am angry that I have to deal with this now. I am so angry that it is hard to keep from beating my head against a wall.

N. S.

* The Combined Action Platoon consisted of American and Vietnamese personnel with a shared command structure. This organization coordinated village defenses and provided medical services for troops and villagers. The CAP mission included trying to become part of village life.

# In Time To Tango

*The Argentine Tango, a hybrid of the old and new worlds, developed out of the poor immigrant quarters of Buenos Aires. A high spirited dance, it quickly became an elegant ballroom dance to a melancholy tune. The man and woman face each other without smiling, staring into infinity. When the beat begins, they hold each other passionately, heads turned in the same direction. They begin a "conversation" that interprets the music. SHE SPEAKS FIRST. He directs while she moves with some resistance into the patterns. THEN HE SPEAKS. Back in a tight embrace, they pull abruptly apart, then carry out the dance until the music ends.*

*A.T.*

40

*In the beginning of fall of 1996 I became a volunteer working with Vietnam vets. The first time I was to co-facilitate a group, I felt some anxiety as to how I would be perceived — a woman, a non-vet. G. early on asked me sharply, "Have you ever been shot at?" Pausing I reflected, finally said, meaning it literally, "only in my dreams." Across the room N's eyes met mine, locked on. During the hour and a half he said little, was obviously thoughtful and reserved. When he did speak, it was an insightful remark or question. Our eyes met again, conveying what? In sessions that followed it seemed that he and I were doing the group together in a point-counterpoint unspoken dialogue, an intelligent duet.*

*A.T.*

words in our teeth
heart in our hands
yellow leaves in the path

no hurry
one foot follows the other

Looking into the Milky Way
Barely far enough
From the lights,
Infinity so clear
The Heavens reach down
To wrench your soul from the
Earth,
Setting you among the Stars
As if you were one of them.
It was that kind of a
Night,
As much in my present now
As it was so many
Years ago.
I was alone,
My back to the earth,
My eyes seeing further than ever
Before,

Deeper than
Ever before.
Sparking the sky as it dug in
Its heels,
Mercury leaping,
This momentary visitor
Skipped to join its fellow wanderers
But fell back, splitting the night again.
Kissing our earth's cheek,
Not shyly, not once, not twice
But five full glorious, passionate times
Before diving into the western ink
In search of some other inevitable
Joining.
Could God love this place
More than I do?

we are all afraid of the night
when a shadow-band of light fades into
blackness
we ache with emptiness
we want to be not alone

last nights full moon was rising
beyond the jagged line of
charcoal

yesterday we walked
marveled at
 snow geese
honking    V-splitting the
pewter sky
down drafted into autumns river
these nine snow birds did in formation fly
            northwest
then wheeling round with updraft
they turned about, joined the chevron
            cutting high

*and twenty geese straight*
*away did fly*
            *south*

*daybreak brings*
            *nightlights*
            *nickel clouds*
            *black crows*
*their raucous voices scavenge the*
            *concrete below*

I, desertman of the dry sea,
Seek solace in the salmon.
When the grief and weariness
Has settled upon me,
I turn to the far long gone
Ocean,
Lurking presence from that
Peaceful past.
How I long for the ocean
To wash over me.
I am kin to the cactus and
Antelope.
Days without water —
The hottest days merely
Temper me.

Yet the salmon calls from
Ancient streams
and tides,
"Become one with me.
Eat and all will be well."
Unknowing, truth irrelevant,
I reply,

"I am yours."
Memories bring me warm,
Clear salt water,
Lifting me, welcoming me home.
Golden days before the end
Can be yours again,
If only you face the ocean.
If only I could be the ocean,
All the years washed white in
Sea foam,
Hung in the breeze to dry into
Old memories,
Cleansed of barbs,

Floating away our pain.
Then we would remember
Pearls that divers
Have brought from the sea.

an owl came to my balcony
in the darkening day
with white ringed eyes
he insisted I had something to
say
words heavy as stones
I spoke
I'm a time traveler finding
the lost pieces
of my life
a kaleidoscope of bits of light
I'm unwinding fields of mind
to the unspoken over there
but never within

I wore my borrowed stones
piedra de la vida  rock of life defiantly
swore I who wore them
would speak the dangerous truth

so protection was granted my gift
my right to witness the
outside world
but never the world within

to see Jaime blue faced
hanging in the cell
to see Julia rocking back and forth
in rot
my right to smell the rancid smell
to cry at each event
to sit by the man who drew
his knife
when the voices commanded him
thus I lost my life over and over
again

who was I who ran
through all the crooked nights
proclaiming my empty gift
I was nobody
had no words
no truth to give
I did not exist
having heard me out
the owl moved his head
to the left then to the right
he dove into darkness
his fading cry was
who is within

Brooding and dark in
Dawn's first beam You said,
"It is not for me
The swallows fly."

Your words rose to meet the
Cock's crow and
I tried to tell you how
Wrong you are.

I have been:
Appealing to the Bible and
God's Universal Love,
Calling on Einstein and his
Song to the Center of
The Universe.
The chorus: $E = MC^2$,
The verse: The Whole of Being can only be
seen from Its Center
and
There you are.

I have been:
Pointing to Paradise in the
desert,
Singing synergies of
Nature
and
Of man.
Watching the garden,
Whispering directly to
Your ear,

" It is for you,
The Swallows fly.

If you are so far away
You cannot see them,

Is that the Swallows fault?"

we each had a sweet dream
you tired of the long wait
me half awake
with a quick glance goodbye
a staccato embrace under sun dappled pine
for a moment our eyes met straight

did you listen to the music
some you muttered
they were I said a gift for your birthday
I did not say I wanted to
give you everything
it was not necessary you knew and I knew
there was nothing we
could do
but turn hearts on our heels
memorize the lingering day

I have hitched my
Wagon to your
Star and
Starred in your fantasy.

What more would
You have of me?
No matter!
For I would bear it,
I would give it,
I would receive it.

Happily,
For that is the
Nature of my love.
This is my trust in you.
 Not to spill this cup
 To see how deep it is.

*moving on*
*green iguana rides your shoulder*
*green on green through jungle growth*
*you weaving your hips to song*
*fluttering humming bird on high*
*in your hand a dusty rose*
*on your lips goodbye*

*for I could not give you everything*
*everything for which you pined*
*I gave you meat  purple plums  and wine*
*a sea of love*
*but still you pined*
*it is not everything*
*the everything you cannot define*

*no I cannot give more*
*and you cannot find*
*in my kiss*
*everything*
*for which you pine*

Take this rock wall
Solid beyond need.
Stronger than any load
That might be
Borne.
Secure in foundation.
Mocking the very weathering
Administered by Father Time.

Inspect this monolith and
Pry forth its secret:

Each stone is its own
Self.
All the mortar fills
Unique strengths.
All the strengths lead to
Unique weakness.

If you
So much as
Pick up the sledgehammer,

You must choose,
Must judge,
Must guess.
Strike
The best blow,
The right angle to begin the
Destruction.

If you
Choose to keep your
Eyes wide open,
How can you fail to
Penetrate the
Mystery
And
What is so different from
This wall and the
One you face?

*María comes over, hugs me and cries, "Que pasó, que pasó." I answer, "No hay cuerpo, ni nada, hueso y carbó n, un explosión, se murió mi hijo."*

*Mother's loud insistent voice mocks me, "I told you to take care of that boy. Why didn't they open the casket?" Inside my head screams, "There's nothing but black and bone."*

*The funeral was like a subdued maypole festival, the breeze and warm birds marking the quiet spring with song. The flowers are blowing on the casket. His friends from the boy scouts are in uniformed attention. A man reads from Thomas Wolfe, Zen, Henry Miller. A girl plays the guitar and sings, "I am a poor wayfaring stranger," that trails off into the morning sky. The bugle clear and implacable cross twenty rows of marble stones. I stand silent feeling nothing, but seeing the military markers and hearing the plaintive tones of Taps:*

  *Day is o'er,*
  *Night is near.*

          *A.T.*

Do not ask me why.
Not one answer exists and
Not one thousand would do.

I could explain about and around
This custom made fit.

Give reasons by the score.
Recite history and herstory,
Hoping to merge them both,
Wary of becoming the mix.

All fall short of why,
Short of expressing love.
All are pale shadows,
Next to our intensity.
Feathers,
Next to our density.
Puddles,
Next to our ocean.

Whole dictionaries thrown
Into that gap would
Never fill or bridge,
Never see from edge to edge.
Never answer that question
You dare not ask.

Cascading patterns yield
bits of light and
bytes of shared
knowledge
painted on our muted canvas
of
confusion and trust.

Points of lustrous color
peek through,
 burst through,
recede and risk being left
unspoken.

Admiration, mine for
you, deep and abiding.
beauty, in person,
in spirit.
Courage, perhaps you don't
even know....
wit and tender wisdom.
Talent.
Compassion.
Lovely green eyes and
scent of your heartbeat.

Yes,
what a desirable woman and
ardent lover you are!

Yet,
There is no answer here...
Accountability escapes,
reason collapses,
leaving, raw and exposed,
my affections and the
simple fact of love.

In 1968 the outside world I thought I knew and the world I believed to have a certain configuration fell apart; my inner personal world turned upside down, altered forever. "Dawn lifts up her shoulder on a long ridge of stone". These lines of Lorca were to become my moribund motif for the years of exile in the wastelands. The train whistle cutting the air cried loneliness, abandonment. The incident was never mentioned, the story never allowed to be told. It was as if my boy never existed. Within me the black vacancy remained unknown for thirty years. My family never went with me to the cemetery. Instead, I was blamed, and I took the guilt on.

A.T.

morning rays fill the scotch
with liquid fire
streak amber into the beat fast then slow
in this new land under molten
fire
music measures hope
fast then slow
step step close
I move to the tango

unspeakable sights skewed
my eyes
terror overrode original terror
that I had lost my home
had been turned away
a refugee with heart of cold

from bedrock of my beginning
my heart beat staccato then
slow
drove me through lands
where Sirens sang songs and
some were left like Sisyphus
forever rolling the stone
under pearl wet skies that
rained forty days and forty
nights
now moving in this evening
of the world
streaking amber into the soul
I listen to the beat
fast then slow
I step step close
in time to tango

In the morning
When your eyes are
Soft and
Before you gather
Your energies to
Face the day,
There is an honest
Moment of
Vulnerability.

The moment becomes a
Lens.
The lens turns upon a
Rare beauty.
I am privileged to witness
and
I am privileged to say,
My treasure of all treasures
Harvested from
Our easy mornings is that
Inviting depth of
Your eyes.

*I was leaving*
*but you said wait*
*you must take this*
*you were right*
*knowing my hunger you*
*filled me*
*with pale green chili jelly*
*fed me on the end of your chopstick*
*pink shrimp*
*strings of vermicelli*
*my love you fill my well*

If you'll be my Lily Pad
I will be your Chicory Flower.
You flower Pearly White.
I'm a Hard Blue.
What will be the
Aroma of this
Distillation?

this emblazoned october
breeze
cannot bring ease
cascading maples cannot
relieve
the too long wait
vermilion leaves carouse
like a thousand fiery tongues
that play over and over the
riff
love destroyed must be
regained
time warped into pain
yes
I want your hands
I want your lips
'though every kiss a tear
'though every touch a tease
and every riff must end

*how then can I admit*
*untimely love*
*let your hungry arms enfold me*
*give it my ample breast*
*while I drift and fall with*
*each red leaf*
*while I fall and tumble into*
*the abyss*
*while I dream and wait for*
*the silence*
*after the riff*

The weld is stronger than either side.
Fear not the spark, my dear,
For we already live within its Fire.

*what does it matter if my love*
*is a mixed*
*blessing*
*combining as I do father*
*son lover*
*as long as I know how lines*
*intersect*
*as long as I don't expect*
*from you*
*a permanent rainbow a pot*
*of gold*

I need to communicate some thoughts I've been having lately. I am angry about how the money was handled. I didn't know about the trust until the girls told me. I have always been excluded from family business. A job has not been an option since I returned from the war. My condition, Post Traumatic Stress Disorder, is real and not "just mental". It involves both brain structure and blood chemistry changes. Disrespect has been palpable from every one of you. I wish I had stood and challenged your assumption that I was a bad person. My anger is hard for me to acknowledge and describe. I can't just throw it away, because it keeps coming back. A more rational me realizes that I need to deal with it in a sensible way. I am angry with you. Is there a possibility of dealing with my anger in a sensible way? Can it be resolved? Can there be forgiveness?

N.S.

perhaps you believe
I don't give you
what you think you need
look in and explore your
reason
before you can enjoy
the wealth of this season
before you decide
to cut off your confusion
it will not end your drive to
repeat
to stumble through the dance
on faltering
feet again and again
if you have the courage
there is wealth enough
that cannot be depleted
that even time will not end

Perhaps, I do not speak aloud,
These "sweet nothings,"
This praise I feel,
Because of greed and
Some poetic conceit.
Saving them until they
Burst forth in a
          Poem.
Then I have something
      Real to believe in,
Some tangible result
        of the
Pleasure and Pain.

*Driving on the mountain road, sunflowers beside me, I screamed and sobbed, my eyes blinded and salty. I accelerated, hoped the car would plunge over the side, smash my splitting chest, but the car drove on - onto the cemetery road. I wandered among the white marble military stones, clutched the sunflowers, but could not find the headstone. Finally I saw a new mount of brown bearing a cardmarker with his name. It was his name.... As I scattered the sunflowers on top, I thought my son is lying below, burned and black.*

*Easter, when I take a basket of colored eggs, kneel down, and lay them carefully around on top of the green ground, I'm thinking, this is how it is in Greece at 12:00 midnight. The Greeks salute each other at banquets by cracking together their Easter eggs and shouting, "Christos anesti! Christ has risen!" But I can't forgive those who live.*

After the Winter Solstice comes dread. Not for the holiday celebrating the death of the old year and the crowning of the new Sun King, but what I know will follow. It infiltrates slowly in January, creeps closer in February...is contained until Easter.

In May I realize the enormity of the destruction. Yet, I am still here when all the rest have left the field. The minutia of my life suffocates me. I must take up pen, clay, glass, paint to transpose, transcend.

A.T.

*our other lives winding*
*down*
*seduced us*
*yet how could we not have*
*known as*
*into the mountains we*
*climbed and talked*
*a little or a lot*
*the sun was warm on the*
*rocks bearing*
*ancient signs*

further we climbed
months like years passed
the autumn days held fast
beneath the pines
watching kindling catch fire
we lay in the cold
your fingers barely brushing the map
of my road
there were no words in that
quiet
power and hope rose
we had a secret we shared
which had been unbearable
alone

*Dearest N.,*

*Before I went to sleep last night, I had so many words I wanted to say to you words of appreciation, of love. Sitting here on the morning balcony overlooking the water in the slip that parallels Clearwater Causeway, I pause . . . I miss you, my darling. I feel your image so present, so comforting yet an intaglio\* distinct on my heart. Que sono felice! Here I am happy with you in my heart.*

*My sweet, I will wait for you.*

*A.T.*

\*The bold cameo speaks, the soft intaglio thinks.

winding the road to angel fire
into the sangre de christo
winding the road
dirtying the snow
singing

      o mio babbino caro
      o my beloved
where am I
where did you hide
winding into the dirty snow of long ago
my feeling is on hold
underneath lies something known

      o mio babbino caro
      o my beloved
you left me so very long ago

By your own hand
You offered me photos
My eye was carried into your past
Looking for some hint of
Who became you.

I saw the flair and tease,
 Red and Platinum and
Black and
Blessed Daring
Looking for the roots of your beauty,
I found only plain desperation
Trapped in tortured
Liberation
If I speak the truth,
Have you now the
Daring to hear?

You are more beautiful now
        Than ever you have been
Before.

the watermelon morning
grabbed my heart
stretched quiet hope
words if spoken
could not tell of
the void you crossed
giving yourself
waiting patiently for me
to admit my hunger
you are the first
you are the last
love

Old Gold.
This gold has worn this form
For years on end.
Drawing eyes to
Beauty,
Enduring,
Endearing.
Only now, must Time be
Recast.

Shape is lost as Metal meets Fire.
Liquid and flowing
Precious substance
Thrown into a void,
Coalesces clutching
Some new jewel in
Some new light.

Same gold,
New life.

*Shards of memory, detritus from the great upheaval: Ash and pumice though cold can be used. We saw destruction felt exhausted, but bent and picked up bits and pieces and began to build.*

# ARDEN ALLOWYN TICE

## Biography

Arden Tice has published essays and poetry since the 1960s when she first moved to Santa Fe, New Mexico. Her chapbooks include Mi Casa Es Su Casa (1967), *Take It And Fake The Rest* (1974), *Wind In My Fist* (1990), *The Augmented Moon* (1994), and *A Naming of Women* (1994).* *Looking for The Frontier* (Vergin Press, 1992) is a collection of some of her published essays and articles.

She taught psychology at El Paso Community College from 1974 until 1981 and was a practicing psychotherapist from 1978 through 1988. Tice lived with Eskimos at Point Barrow, Alaska before Alaska became a state. She visited and wrote about the Tarahumara Indians in Mexico during the 1960s, and has traveled in Greece, Spain, Costa Rica and China. She was a busy and productive social activist during the '60's and early '70s. In Santa Fe, while working for the Juvenile Probation Department, she set up Parolees El Vicio, a methadone maintenance program and a twenty-four hour youth crisis center for which she wrote the grant and administered until permanent staff came on board.

While living on the border at El Paso and Juarez, she wrote poems in Spanish for barrio protest marches, and was Social Services Director of a large social action program addressing problems of health, housing and food distribution. Much to the chagrin of the warden and the guards, Tice was assigned as the first woman to present instruction to the convicts at La Tuna Federal Penitentiary.

Tice has presented poetry and writing workshops at the University of California (Writer's Week, 1986), Riverside Community College (1987) , as well as other universities, churches, clubs, etc., in New Mexico, California and Texas. Today Tice volunteers in a writing workshop with veterans of the Vietnam War.

Her collected works and papers are archived in the University of New Mexico's Center for Southwest Research.

*All chapbooks of poetry are under 40 pages.

# NICHOLS S. SANDS

## Biography

Nichols S. Sands, a lifelong resident of New Mexico, served in Vietnam 1970-71, as a Hospital Corpsman 2nd class with Marine Combined Action Platoons (CAP) 1-4-6, 1-4-1, 1-1-1, and 1-3-2 in Quang Ngai Province, Republic of Vietnam. CAP 1-4-1 was located at Son My Refugee Ville wherein lived the survivors of the My Lai Massacre and other destroyed villages. Sands also served with the 5th Communications Battalion and the 6th Radio Battalion in Da Nang.

In addition to the military duties as corpsman, Sands conducted over 100 MEDCAPS for Vietnamese civilians, tending them for wounds, standing by them as they died, and grieving afterward for all deaths in that war. The people he was charged with tending were often Viet Cong thus each day and each night contained a very real possibility of betrayal and death at the hands of those he considered friendly.

Although Nichols Sands suffered from chronic and interminable Post Traumatic Stress Disorder (PTSD) since his tour in Vietnam, it was not until 1996 that his illness was acknowledged with a 100% disability declaration from the Veterans Administration. PTSD is a sinister disorder which can destroy personal relationships, as well as destroy one's sense of self value and self esteem. it brings the horrifying past into the present, and can often cause the person to behave in self-destructive and very strange ways...all in an effort to protect oneself from threats of the past. As well as passing through two destroyed marriages and suffering a marred family life, Sands became one of the "country" homeless who found shelter in sheds, shacks, chicken coops and other shadowed niches of our society.

Since his time in Vietnam, Nichols Sands concentrated on learning to live with PTSD. Creativity has been one of the major ways he has learned to cope. He has been a jeweler whose work is known for its unique combination of contemporary design with native stones, and in 1998 he began creating jewel-like *meditation windows* that are now featured in many private collections. Additionally, Sands is a skilled machinist, artist, and a poet whose grasp of life's stark realities is sometimes unnerving and always poignant. He has participated in several writing groups and, in 1998, worked with Arden Tice to establish an ongoing veterans' writing group.

Prior to going to Vietnam, Sands completed one year of college at the University of New Mexico and another year and a half after his return. His major interest was in art and economics. Later, he attended trade school studying as a machinist.

His written works have been published in various magazines including *Life Fish: selected poems* (1986), *Poetry and the Vietnam Experience,* Saint Lawrence University (1987), and *The Rio Grande Writers Quarterly* (1986).

Authors Arden Tice and Nichols Sands met in Albuquerque, New Mexico when they started a Veterans' writing group.

Arden Tice has been publishing essays, articles and chapbooks of poetry since the 1960s when she came to Santa Fe. Robert Graves had written her saying she was a fine poet, when she wasn't writing like all the "beats." She continued writing and was an involved social activist throughout the 1960s and 1970s. She has worked with the Eskimos of Barrow, Alaska, the people in the barrios on the border and the Tarahumara Indians of the Sierra Madre Mountains of Mexico.

Nichols Sands has published his poems since he returned from Vietnam. His contemporary New Mexican jewelry, original and beautiful, had to be abandoned because of his disability. Recently he created striking colorful "jeweled meditation windows" of glass.

## *Ordering Information*

*Call your order to (505) 242-1838*

*Email: nicholssands@aol.com*
*or*
*ardentice@spinn.net*

*or fax it to (505) 242-7697*

*or write to:*

*P.O. Box 7403*
*Albuquerque, NM 87194*

*or*

*VERGIN PRESS*
*P.O. BOX 370322*
*EL PASO, TEXAS 79937*